Contemporary Native Americans
LaDonna Harris

BY
MICHAEL SCHWARTZ

RAINTREE
STECK-VAUGHN
PUBLISHERS
The Steck-Vaughn Company

Austin, Texas

Copyright © 1997, Steck-Vaughn Company. All rights reserved. No part of this book may be reproduced or utilized in any form or by any means, electronic or mechanical, including photocopying, recording, or by any information storage and retrieval system, without permission in writing from the copyright owner. Requests for permission to make copies of any part of the work should be mailed to: Copyright Permissions, Steck-Vaughn Company, P.O. Box 26015, Austin, Texas 78755.

Published by Raintree Steck-Vaughn, an imprint of Steck-Vaughn Company.
Produced by Mega-Books, Inc.
Design and Art Direction by Michaelis/Carpelis Design Associates.
Cover photo: Dick Ruddy

Library of Congress Cataloging-in-Publication Data
Schwartz, Michael.
 LaDonna Harris / by Michael Schwartz.
  p. cm. — (Contemporary Native Americans)
 Includes bibliographical references (p. 47) and index.
 Summary: Explores the life and accomplishments of LaDonna Harris, the Comanche woman who spent many years working for the rights of Native Americans.
 ISBN 0-8172-3995-2 (Hardcover)
 ISBN 0-8172-6884-7 (Softcover)
 1. Harris, LaDonna—Juvenile literature. 2. Comanche Indians—Biography—Juvenile literature. 3. Oklahoma—Biography—Juvenile literature. 4. Indians of North America—Government relations—Juvenile literature. [1. Harris, LaDonna. 2. Comanche Indians—Biography. 3. Indians of North America—Oklahoma—Biography.]
I. Title. II. Series.
E99.C85H287 1997
976.6'0049745—dc21   96-44089
[B]   CIP
                                        AC
Printed and bound in the United States.

1 2 3 4 5 6 7 8 9 LB 00 99 98 97 96

Photo credits: Courtesy of U. S. Department of Energy: p. 4; ©Gene Peach Photography/Liaison International: p. 7; ©Forsyth/Monkmeyer: p. 8; Corbis-Bettmann: p. 11; The Bettmann Archive: p.13; Courtesy of Americans for Indian Opportunity: pp. 14, 16, 29, 33, 34, 37, 39, 41, 42, 45; AP/Wide World Photos: pp. 19, 31; UPI/Bettmann: p. 20; UPI/Corbis-Bettmann: pp. 23, 24, 26.

Contents

1 The Story of Blue Lake 5

2 One Girl, Two Cultures 10

3 Opportunity for Everyone 17

4 Next Stop: Washington 25

5 A Friend to Presidents 32

6 Reaching Out 38

Important Dates 46

Glossary 47

Bibliography 47

Index 48

Chapter

THE STORY OF BLUE LAKE

LaDonna Harris leaned into the microphone. She looked into the audience at the faces of United States senators. Her husband, Senator Fred R. Harris of Oklahoma, sat nearby. LaDonna was the wife of a senator, but the opinions and arguments she was about to present were her own. This was a historic moment. Never before had a senator's wife spoken before a Senate committee.

In the past, wives and husbands of senators had remained silent about government policies, but in December 1970, LaDonna wanted to be heard. She intended to convince the senators that the United States government should return Blue Lake to the Taos Pueblo Indians of New Mexico. She knew that

LaDonna Harris is a powerful public speaker. Her speeches are so effective in part because she believes in the causes she fights for.

at least one powerful senator disagreed with her, but LaDonna was not afraid.

LaDonna Harris was the perfect choice to speak before the committee. She belonged to the Comanche tribe and had spent many years working with Native American tribes all over North America. By 1970, 39-year-old LaDonna had already formed Oklahomans for Indian Opportunity (OIO), a group that had united more than 60 tribes in her home state. Because of her experience with OIO, she knew how important it was for tribes to have a voice in the United States government. She also knew how important it was for their voice to be heard.

All eyes turned to her, and with her words and presence, LaDonna commanded the senators' attention and respect. Her appearance was striking. Like her Comanche mother, she had beautiful black hair and a rich, dark complexion. Like her father, who was of Irish descent, she had blue eyes. Like her Comanche grandparents, she knew how to speak both powerfully and from the heart.

LaDonna explained to the senators how many Native American tribes faced such serious problems as poverty and poor health care. She made it clear that before the tribes could overcome these problems, the government needed to give them back the land that was rightfully theirs. Then after LaDonna spoke, more experts testified before the committee. Soon the senators would vote and make a decision.

▲ Taos Pueblo village in New Mexico. The Taos Pueblo Indians have lived in adobe homes in this region for hundreds of years.

For centuries the Taos Pueblo Indians had lived in small villages scattered throughout the Sangre de Cristo Mountains in north-central New Mexico. They farmed, raised animals, and took care of the land around beautiful Blue Lake.

In the 1700s, when Spanish settlers entered the territory, the Taos people were still able to live peacefully with the settlers. The two groups even shared their cultures and customs with each other. Many of the Taos people had adopted the Christian religion of the Spanish settlers.

Things changed drastically in 1906. In that year the United States government took control of 48,000 acres of Taos Pueblo land, including Blue Lake. For

Blue Lake in New Mexico. Largely due to LaDonna Harris's speech to the Senate committee, Blue Lake was returned to the Taos Pueblo Indians.

years the Indians watched silently as campers littered the land with garbage. They watched as ranchers let their cattle strip the land of vegetation. Though the lake was sacred to the Taos people, they could not even travel to it without first obtaining a permit from the government.

The Indians tried for years to win back Blue Lake, but few would listen. At least not until LaDonna Harris raised her voice to convince the government to do what was right.

"LaDonna gets very involved with people and with the step-by-step details of getting something done," observes her former husband, Fred R. Harris. "She talked to all the senators of the subcommittee personally. She talked to the people in the White House at the time. In the end the government changed its policy, and I'd say the reason was LaDonna."

In December 1970 Congress voted to return Blue Lake to the Taos Pueblo Indians. When they heard the news, the Taos Pueblo celebrated. They had struggled for almost 75 years, and now they had won. Their voices had finally been heard.

Following this change, President Richard Nixon declared that the United States should improve its policies toward Native Americans. He said that the rights of Native American tribes to keep their land would be given more respect and protection.

LaDonna Harris was happy, too. The victory was not just for the Taos Pueblo Indians—it was a victory for Native Americans all over the country.

The story of Blue Lake is just one example of how LaDonna Harris has fought for the rights of Native Americans. LaDonna has devoted her whole adult life to helping tribes work together for a better future. Her life is an inspiration to many people. She has shown that with courage and hard work, one person can make a big difference in the world.

Chapter Two

ONE GIRL, TWO CULTURES

LaDonna Harris was born LaDonna Crawford in Temple, Oklahoma, in 1931. Her mother was a Comanche Indian; her father was Irish American. While growing up, LaDonna says, she always felt as if she belonged to two worlds—the Indian world and the white world.

The area that is now the state of Oklahoma has been home to these two very different cultures for centuries. When European settlers came to North America, several tribes, including the Comanche and the Kiowa, were living in the western part of the area. The Caddo, the Wichita, and the Pawnee lived in the eastern part.

In 1819 the United States government decided that this whole area was a good place to relocate Native American tribes from other parts of the country. This decision was made in order to make room for the European settlers who were coming to live in the United States. In the late 1830s, 15,000 Native

Americans were forced to walk from eastern states to the new territory against their will. Because of hunger and disease, many people died along the way. This journey later became known as the Trail of Tears.

At first the Native Americans were given most of the land in the area, which the government divided into reservations. A reservation is an area of land set aside by the United States government for Native Americans to live on. But as the years went on, white settlers began to see the land as a good place to live because of its rich soil.

By 1905 there were five times as many whites as

An artist's painting of the Trail of Tears, a time during the early 1800s when thousands of Native Americans were relocated to Oklahoma against their will.

Native Americans in the territory. Before the United States government made Oklahoma a state in 1907, it took back the land from the tribes and gave it to the white settlers who were moving there from the East.

The name given to the new state, Oklahoma, reflects the state's roots. It is a combination of two Choctaw words—*okla*, which means "people," and *homma*, which means "red." (During that time period, Native Americans were called "redskins" by whites because their skin seemed more red than white. Today this term is recognized as offensive and cruel and is no longer accepted by society.)

Despite the fact that Native Americans had been treated unfairly by the government, they worked hard to live side by side in peace with the new settlers. The official state seal, which was created in 1907, shows a white frontiersman and a Native American shaking hands. The symbol was meant to show cooperation between the two cultures.

Even so the people of these two cultures did not live equally. White settlers were given better land to farm. As a result they produced better goods and had more opportunities to make money. By contrast Native Americans became very poor.

At the time, the United States government was making laws to force Native Americans around the country to shed their own cultures and adopt "white" ways. Native American children were often sent away from home to government-run boarding schools.

An abandoned farm near Guymon, Oklahoma. During the Great Depression, the land in Oklahoma and other states dried up, partly due to a drought. Unable to plant crops, the farmers were forced to move.

There they were sometimes beaten if they spoke their own languages instead of English.

By the 1930s life had not become any easier for the Native Americans of Oklahoma. In fact life was not easy for anyone, Indian or white, because of the Great Depression. The Great Depression was a time when many people all over the country lost their jobs and their savings. In Oklahoma things were even worse.

A terrible drought, or long period without rain, combined with a series of terrible dust storms, turned 50 million acres of land in Oklahoma, Colorado, Kansas, New Mexico, and Texas into a dried-up wasteland. People nicknamed this part of the country "the Dust Bowl." Farms were destroyed. With no crops, people were in danger of starving. They left Oklahoma by the thousands and headed for California and other western states.

This was the Oklahoma where LaDonna grew up. When she was a baby, her parents separated. Her father left, hoping to find work in California. He never returned. Her mother remained in Oklahoma to work at the hospital in Fort Sill, a nearby army base. In those days women working at the hospital were expected to live on hospital grounds. So LaDonna was raised by her mother's parents on a small farm outside

LaDonna in 1939 when she was eight years old. With her are her hardworking mother, Lilly Crawford, and her proud, traditional grandmother, Wick-kie.

the town of Walters, Oklahoma. For the first four years of her life, LaDonna spoke only Comanche, the language of her grandparents.

During these rough times, LaDonna's grandfather, Tibbytite, and her grandmother, Wick-kie, managed to keep their farm running. LaDonna has very happy memories of her childhood. For fun she would go horseback riding or play in the cool waters of the creek. She also helped her grandparents by gathering eggs and watering plants. LaDonna remembers that her grandmother always wore long braids and traditional Comanche ankle-length skirts and shawls. Wick-kie taught LaDonna the language, traditions, and stories of the Comanche people.

"LaDonna's grandmother was one of the most marvelous, charming, and clever people I've ever known," remembers Fred Harris.

LaDonna recalls listening to her grandfather's stories. He was an Eagle Medicine Man, or healer. When he was a boy, Tibbytite was sent to a government boarding school. He resisted the authorities who tried to make him give up his Comanche ways. When they tried to cut off his long black braids, he ran away from the school.

When LaDonna was old enough to go to school, her life changed drastically. She attended a white school near the farm and learned English. Unlike children at the school Tibbytite went to, LaDonna wasn't forced to give up her traditions. Still, white children teased

LaDonna (center), seen with her mother and grandmother in 1972. LaDonna felt her childhood exposed her to the best of both white and Comanche worlds.

and insulted her because she was Native American. LaDonna remembers how the teachers treated her differently than they treated the white students. It hurt.

Looking back, LaDonna says her childhood helped shape the course her life would take. Because of her experiences, she has said that she "views life with the wisdom and values of two cultures." The love and support of the Comanche community gave her the strength to overcome the obstacles she would face in the white world.

As a Comanche, she knew the problems that the native people of Oklahoma faced. She also realized that for other Americans the United States offered many opportunities. She thought Oklahoma's Native Americans deserved the same opportunities as the other residents of Oklahoma. LaDonna decided to devote her life to changing the lives of Native Americans.

Chapter Three

OPPORTUNITY FOR EVERYONE

While she was growing up, LaDonna had met someone who would help her achieve her vision of **equality** for Native Americans—Fred Harris.

Fred and LaDonna were neighbors and high-school classmates in Walters, Oklahoma. They met when they were both sophomores. Fred's family, according to their daughter Laura Harris, were "dirt-poor sharecroppers." Fred's father traded cattle, but he did not own any farmland himself.

Fred was a good student. He dreamed of attending the University of Oklahoma and then law school. He hoped to go into politics someday. He had seen how President Franklin Roosevelt had given new hope to farmers and poor families during the Great Depression. President Roosevelt's policies had brought electricity to rural areas, created jobs, and supported people in need. Fred wanted to make a difference in people's lives just as President Roosevelt had done.

When Fred and LaDonna began to date, Fred became interested in her culture. He had a great respect for LaDonna's grandparents. LaDonna began to teach Fred the Comanche language and traditions. Fred and LaDonna married in 1949, after they graduated from high school.

LaDonna and Fred knew that a good education would help Fred enter politics. Fred began his studies at Oklahoma State University. Between classes and after school he worked as a printer. LaDonna made money by providing daytime care in their home for neighborhood children. They lived in a small village of mobile homes near the university.

LaDonna worked in the library of the University of Oklahoma, which was also nearby. LaDonna was very good at her work, and a year later she took a better job in the university's Office of Continuing Education. Fred and LaDonna worked hard as partners so that they could achieve their dreams together.

In 1954 their hard work began to pay off. Fred became a lawyer, and they moved to Lawton, a city in southwest Oklahoma near the Texas border. There Fred began his legal practice. Two years later Fred took another big step. In 1956, with LaDonna's help, he ran for the office of Oklahoma state senator. He ran as a Democrat and won.

The Harrises thought of politics not just as a career or as a way to make money. For Fred and LaDonna, politics was a way to make their state a better place in

Senator Fred Harris, LaDonna's high-school sweetheart and husband, who became a politician to make a difference as President Roosevelt had during the Great Depression.

which to live and to change laws that caused problems. In the 1950s some of these problematic laws discriminated against people who were not white.

Oklahoma and other parts of the United States had laws that enforced a practice called segregation. Under segregation people who were not considered "white" could not do certain things. They could not eat in certain restaurants. They had to sit in separate sections of trains and buses. They could not use rest rooms and drinking fountains that were reserved for whites only. In some states children of different races were not even allowed to go to school together.

In the 1950s the United States began to do away with segregation. A minister named Martin Luther King, Jr., led protests, made speeches, went to jail, and eventually was killed for what he believed in. Dr. King believed that African Americans and people of all races deserved to live as equals in the United States. He said that by working together in peace, people could change the unjust policies of the government. Millions of people joined Dr. King's fight for equal rights, which was called the Civil Rights Movement. People held meetings and walked in nonviolent marches and protests. They made their voices heard.

In Lawton, where LaDonna and Fred lived,

A picture of the March on Washington, August 28, 1963. The Reverend Dr. Martin Luther King, Jr., who spoke at this Civil Rights protest, taught LaDonna the importance of having people work together as a group.

segregation was common. They became active in civil rights work in Oklahoma. LaDonna worked with a citizens' group, and Fred served as a member of the mayor's committee to **integrate** restaurants, swimming pools, and other public places.

From Dr. King, LaDonna learned how important it was for people to stand together as a group. With Fred in the state senate, LaDonna now knew how to work within the government's system to make changes.

Fred Harris remembers that "LaDonna took part in the Civil Rights efforts in a personal way." LaDonna organized a group that met once a week. Half of the group was African American, the other half of the group was white. Each week they would meet in a different home. One week the group would gather in an African-American home, the next week they would meet in a white home.

Together the members of the group worked to end segregation. They stood with protest signs outside a swimming pool that was segregated. They protested at selected restaurants, demanding that these businesses serve people of all races.

LaDonna was also concerned about women. In the 1950s women weren't allowed to serve on court juries in Oklahoma. They were generally kept out of politics. Fred remembers how as a politician on the campaign trail, he would ask for women's votes. Often women would say, "I don't know about politics. I let my husband take care of that."

LaDonna wanted to help women participate in their country's government. She joined a women's organization concerned with public affairs and was an early pioneer in what later became known as the Women's Movement.

LaDonna's visibility in politics often drew criticism from people who thought women belonged only in the home. Many people at that time thought that women should only concern themselves with cooking, cleaning, and taking care of children.

But LaDonna was most involved in the many troubles faced by Native Americans. In the 1960s many Indians lived in poverty and poor health. At a time when the average person in the United States could expect to live to age 65, Native Americans could expect to live only to age 43.

LaDonna knew it was important for Indians to have a voice in the government so they could address their problems. But at that time, the tribes did not speak with one voice. They needed to come together to meet and organize. In 1964 LaDonna and other leaders decided to bring together tribes from all over Oklahoma to discuss their problems and share information about what they could do.

"We didn't know what to expect," LaDonna remembers. "We didn't know if anyone would come, or if they would participate. It was the first time in the 20th century that eastern and western Oklahoma tribes had ever met together."

A Cherokee Indian boy swings over his family's rundown porch in 1969. Most Native Americans in the 1960s lived in poverty-stricken and overcrowded homes such as this one.

The gathering was a huge success. Representatives from 68 tribes throughout the state came to share their knowledge and experience. They realized that they could learn from each other, work together, and help each other. LaDonna decided that the time was right to form a permanent organization dedicated to solving the problems of Native Americans in her state. This is how the Oklahomans for Indian Opportunity (OIO) was formed.

The tribes rallied around LaDonna's plan. More than 60 tribes joined to form Oklahomans for Indian Opportunity. The goal of OIO was to create **economic opportunity** for the tribes. Native Americans were the poorest of the poor in the nation. Many didn't have

Leaders of the first Grand Council of the American Indian, 1963. From left to right: Frank Tompee-Saw (Cherokee), Fighting Bear Rickard (Tuscadora), Emelina Escobar de Aragon (Zepoteca), Chief Loudvoice Rickard (President of the Indian Defense League), Margaret Wilber (Menominee), and Chief Lightfoot Talking Eagle (Susquenock).

enough money to buy food and clothing. They lived without electricity or running water. With the right kind of help from the government, the tribes could start businesses and sell their goods. LaDonna knew that this was the first step toward making the tribes strong.

The creation of OIO was an amazing achievement. There were no other government funded organizations for Native Americans like it in the country. LaDonna Harris had started something big—something that would only become more powerful. It was the beginning of a new era for Native Americans in the United States.

Chapter *Four*

NEXT STOP: WASHINGTON

While LaDonna Harris was running OIO, Fred Harris was busy with his political career. In 1964 Fred ran for office again. This time he was aiming for the United States Senate. Like President Lyndon Johnson, who won the 1964 presidential election in a **landslide**, Fred was a Democrat. Fred's vocal support of Civil Rights was popular with many voters. Once again Fred won. Now he was spending half of the year working in Washington, D.C. As a United States senator, Fred helped write and approve laws for the whole nation instead of just for Oklahoma.

The Harris family moved to Virginia, to a town that was just outside of Washington, D.C. LaDonna's daughter, Laura, remembers how exciting it was to grow up in a political family. "I grew up at a table constantly filled with talk of politics and Civil Rights and other issues of the time," Laura says. "We always had dinner together, though it was often late in the

Fred points out a few of the city's sights to LaDonna from the steps of the Capitol Building in Washington, D.C. When Fred became a U.S. senator, they moved to the Washington, D.C. area to live.

evening because of my parents' schedules."

From the beginning, LaDonna took to life in Washington, D.C. She instantly showed her talent for getting involved, making friends, and working for causes that she believed in. Her first opportunity came at a meeting of the Senate Wives Club.

Traditionally the wives of senators met in a club to talk and make plans to raise money for charities. The first time LaDonna attended a meeting was special because new members were introduced. Lady Bird Johnson, the president's wife, made an appearance. LaDonna had been seated with the younger and newest club members at that meeting. One of those members was Ethel Kennedy, the wife of Senator Robert F. Kennedy, who had served as United States **attorney general** for his brother, President John F. Kennedy.

According to Fred Harris, Ethel Kennedy felt very shy at this meeting. She confessed to LaDonna in a whisper, "I don't know anyone."

LaDonna smiled at her and said, "Kid, I don't know any of these people either." This was the beginning of a friendship between the Harris and Kennedy families.

LaDonna soon learned that one of the activities of the Senate Wives Club was to meet in the basement of the Russell Senate Office building once a week, put on blue uniforms, and roll bandages for the Red Cross. LaDonna, Ethel Kennedy, and other senators' wives, such as Joan Mondale and Marvela Bayh, began to ask each other, "Is rolling bandages the best use of our time?"

These women began to discuss important issues of the day and to invite speakers to address the club. Individually, LaDonna and other senators' wives began to take public stands on issues that mattered to them. For LaDonna that meant becoming involved in promoting and protecting Native American rights.

As a senator's wife, LaDonna kept her eyes and ears open. She had learned how to work with the state government to make changes in Oklahoma. Now she had an opportunity to learn how the federal government worked. In 1964 LaDonna was proud to be part of President Johnson's War on Poverty. This was not really a war, but a call for new laws to help poor families improve their lives through education and job training, and to fund food and housing programs.

LaDonna wanted to help convince the government to assist Native Americans with these programs. She wanted her organization, OIO, to be able to offer programs that would bring jobs and other aid to Indian communities. First she had to learn to use her writing skills to describe what kind of help was needed. Next she had to use her public speaking skills to convince the government that the new programs would benefit Native Americans.

Fred Harris shared his wife's dream of opportunity for Native Americans. Together they formed a powerful team in the nation's capital. They worked hard to make changes in laws and policies that were harmful and unfair to Native Americans.

LaDonna knew how to bring people together as a team. She had learned through her work in Oklahoma that teamwork was the best way to achieve a big change. Once her team had written a proposal, or formal suggestion, for a new program, LaDonna had several people read the proposal and find ways to make it even better. The result was usually a successful proposal that helped OIO receive money and assist more people.

One change LaDonna and Fred helped make was to persuade Congress to give Blue Lake back to the Taos Pueblos in 1970. In 1973 they had another big victory, one that involved fighting a policy called Termination.

Fred and LaDonna meet with Native Americans during the 1976 presidential race.

In the early 1950s, the United States government had decided to terminate the status of some native tribes. This meant that under federal law the tribe would no longer be considered a tribe.

Tribes that were terminated lost their land and any other resources the government had agreed to give them years ago. The government said that in order for tribes to become self-sufficient, they should cut all ties with the government and assimilate, or become absorbed, into the white world.

The government claimed that Termination had given tribes freedom. But many people, like LaDonna and Fred, saw that Termination was unfair. In many cases the government had used Termination to take away valuable land so the government could profit from it. The tribes, in turn, had been left with nothing.

On July 8, 1970, President Richard Nixon delivered a special message to Congress. He said that no longer could any tribe be terminated against its wishes. President Nixon's declaration made some members of Congress unhappy, but the president felt strongly that he was doing the right thing. He believed that the national government had an obligation to help Native Americans become independent and successful without losing the sense of community that tribes provided. After President Nixon's message, Navajo leader Peter MacDonald said that the president should be viewed as "the Abraham Lincoln of the Native American people."

President Nixon's policy ended unfair Termination. But what about the tribes that had already been terminated and had their land taken away? Shouldn't someone help them?

LaDonna came to the aid of one tribe, the Menominee of Wisconsin. Almost 4,000 people made up this tribe when the government terminated it in 1961. More than 200,000 acres of land were taken from them. LaDonna and Fred decided to take the Menominee's fight to the nation's capital. In 1973 Congress restored the Menominee's tribal status. The tribe regained its rights as well as some of its land.

The rulings in the cases of the Taos Pueblo and the Menominee Indians helped change government policies.

Governor Patrick J. Lucey of Wisconsin signing the bill that returned lands to the Menominee Indians. LaDonna and Fred fought to restore the tribal status of the Menominee Indians.

As a result, new laws were made that still guide Native American policy today.

While LaDonna was busy urging Congress to change the unfair laws, she never lost her vision of bringing tribes together to work for change. Oklahomans for Indian Opportunity was running successfully. Why couldn't the same idea work on a national level?

Chapter Five

A FRIEND TO PRESIDENTS

LaDonna took the basic idea of OIO and formed Americans for Indian Opportunity (AIO) in 1970. With this large organization, LaDonna had higher goals than ever before.

One important goal of AIO was to work with Native American youths to help them learn about and gain pride in their culture. LaDonna spent a lot of time studying the problems of Native American children. She noticed that many seemed to do well in school until they reached adolescence. LaDonna believes that it is around this period that Native American children learn about discrimination and how poorly their people have been treated throughout history.

"These children would often say, 'Things must be my fault,'" LaDonna says. "'Maybe I'm not a good person because my family's life is so hard.'" It became very important to LaDonna to help Native Americans become aware of the reasons for their circumstances and to help them develop more positive self-images.

By founding AIO, LaDonna wanted to build partnerships. She hoped that the tribes would work together for a better future. She also hoped that Native Americans and non-Native Americans would work together to understand and help each other.

Through AIO she has worked to strengthen tribal governments and help tribes share traditional Native American ways of resolving disputes. She has developed a program called the Tribal Issues Management System. Through this program she has helped the Winnebago, the Poarch Band Creek, the Oklahoma Apache, the Cheyenne-Arapaho, the

LaDonna Harris (center) at a protest march for Native American rights in Marquette, Michigan, 1971.

Comanche, the Pawnee, and the Menominee return to forms of government that were used centuries ago by their tribal ancestors.

LaDonna's hard work and good ideas have never been ignored. Throughout the 1960s and 1970s and into the 1990s, LaDonna's achievements have been recognized by several presidents of the United States.

Presidents often set up committees to work on important national issues. LaDonna has worked on a number of committees for five presidents in her lifetime. It is a great honor to be asked to join a presidential committee. It is an opportunity to shape national laws that will affect so many.

LaDonna (left) and her grandmother Wick-kie are seen with Lady Bird Johnson, then First Lady of the United States, and Speaker of the House Carl Albert in 1964.

LaDonna became a familiar face in Washington, D.C., after Fred was elected to Congress in 1964. President Lyndon B. Johnson, also elected that year, was the first president to recognize LaDonna's abilities. He asked her to serve on the National Council for Indian Opportunity. It was a perfect place for LaDonna, and she served on the committee for several years.

Since then LaDonna has served on other committees for Presidents Nixon, Ford, Carter, and Clinton. Through this work she has helped the Environmental Protection Agency, the Department of Agriculture, and the Department of Energy set up national policies to improve the lives of Native Americans.

In the early 1970s, the Women's Movement began seeking equal rights for women. LaDonna became one of the first members of the National Women's Political Caucus, an organization founded to work for improving women's lives through political change.

One of the issues the group addressed was equal rights for women in the workplace. Women often got paid much less money for doing the same jobs that men did. The caucus wanted laws passed that would end this kind of discrimination. Because of LaDonna's work with the National Women's Political Caucus and her other achievements, President Gerald Ford named LaDonna as a member of the U.S. Commission on the Observance of International Women's Year in 1974.

By 1979 presidents were not the only people aware of LaDonna's impressive accomplishments. The national magazine *Ladies' Home Journal* named LaDonna "Woman of the Year and of the Decade." Millions of Americans were introduced to the woman who had worked behind the scenes for so many years to improve the lives of all kinds of people.

In 1980 she was nominated by the Citizen's Party as its candidate for Vice President of the United States. She was selected principally because of her leadership in the Native American community. The Citizen's Party also nominated LaDonna because of her vision on other issues, such as protection of the environment, women's rights, and civil rights.

As a Comanche, LaDonna holds the traditional belief that the Earth is sacred and people should take care of it. By the 1970s many people noticed that the Earth was being harmed by pollution in the air, in the water, and on land. LaDonna's belief in the importance of nature came from her grandparents and all the other people who had helped her when she was growing up.

In the Native American community, LaDonna is known not only for starting AIO, but also for starting several other important Native American organizations, including the National Indian Housing Council, the National Tribal Environmental Council, the Council of Energy Resource Tribes, and the National Indian Business Association.

LaDonna remains proud of her first national organization, the AIO. It is as much a success now

LaDonna Harris shares the spotlight with Senate Majority Leader Bob Dole (center) and Senator Morris Udall, around 1984.

as when it started. She has served as president of the organization at its headquarters in Bernalillo, New Mexico, for almost three decades. Even now LaDonna's work is far from complete. She never lets the glamour of Washington, D.C., take her mind off the people she cares about.

"When I give a talk," LaDonna says, "I always notice who comes up to shake my hand afterward. Almost always all the Indians come. As long as they do, then I know I am still all right."

Chapter *Six*

REACHING OUT

Today LaDonna lives and works in Bernalillo, New Mexico. She and Fred divorced in 1981 but remain close friends. They even continue to work together on projects that are important to both of them. Their children are all grown. Their older daughter, Kathryn Tijerina, is the Cultural Services Director for the city of Albuquerque, New Mexico. Their son, Byron, works for a television production company. Their younger daughter, Laura, serves as Projects Director of AIO and frequently travels with her mother on business for AIO.

LaDonna has seen her children grow and change over the years. She has seen the lives of Native Americans grow and change as well. Today almost 50 percent of Native Americans in the United States live on reservations. Many tribes have overcome some of the obstacles they faced in the 1960s, but for others there is still a long way to go. Native Americans who live on reservations are still some of the poorest people in the United States. LaDonna feels that the main struggle for many of these people is to find ways to succeed economically without losing their identities as members of tribes.

To help Native Americans meet these challenges, LaDonna travels all over the country. She visits tribes and talks to government officials about building partnerships together. Back in New Mexico, she works with AIO on several important projects.

LaDonna is convinced that to solve their problems, Native Americans need more leaders. They need leaders who will bring together people from within each tribe and from the tribal governments and the

LaDonna at a gathering of Native American ambassadors in New Mexico, 1993, with Michael Tsosie, a Navajo, on her left.

federal government. For this reason AIO established the American Indian Ambassadors Program, a national Native American leadership training program.

"Its purpose is to develop a new generation of Native American leaders," says Laura Harris, who helps supervise the program.

The program selects members of the Native American community between the ages of 25 and 35 to become ambassadors for a year. An ambassador is an official representative of a country or, in this case, of the Native American community. Not only do the ambassadors come from different tribes, the group is also made up of people who have different occupations—artists, police officers, doctors, lawyers, and so on. Laura Harris says, "We do that on purpose because we think that leadership emerges from many walks of life."

Each year the program invites the ambassadors to Washington, D.C., to meet with government officials, learn how the federal government works, and find ways that they can make their voices heard. The ambassadors also visit tribes that have successful tribal governments, such as the Menominee in Wisconsin and the Makah tribe in the state of Washington.

The Native American Ambassadors Program also works to help the ambassadors use tribal values in the modern world. The AIO defines tribal values with four words: *relationships, responsibility, reciprocity,* and *redistribution.* "Relationships" refers to the importance

LaDonna at a Native American telecommunications meeting, Denver, Colorado, in December 1993. With her are Andrew Jennes (Grande Rhonde), James May (Kootenai Cherokee), and Madonna Yawakie (Chippewa).

of the relationships tribe members have with their families and with their tribes. Tribe members have a responsibility to take care of the people they have relationships with. Within each relationship, there is also reciprocity, which means that the responsibilities are two-way responsibilities. In other words, tribe members should take care of their families and tribe, and their families and tribe should also take care of them. Redistribution means that the amount of money and belongings that tribe members have should be fair. Nobody should go hungry, and nobody should have too much.

To help those who are already leaders in their tribes, the AIO holds leadership workshops. These

LaDonna's concern for native peoples extends across the borders of the United States. In December 1993, LaDonna met with officials from an Otomi Indian tribe in Mexico.

workshops help leaders to address the issues facing their tribes and help them resolve conflicts.

Another project takes the AIO to the people and tribes of Central and South America. Native Americans in the United States have made great strides over the years. LaDonna knows that native tribes in other parts of the world are facing the same struggles that Native Americans have faced in the past. These tribes are in danger of losing their identities or of being terminated. Their customs, traditions, and languages are in danger of being wiped out or lost forever. The AIO hopes to help keep those tribes alive and strong.

Here in the United States, the AIO is keeping an

eye on the future. Now Native Americans have a place to call their own on the information superhighway, or the Internet. The AIO has created the first Indian-owned-and-operated computer network—INDIANnet.

LaDonna developed the idea for INDIANnet in the early 1990s. She knows that knowledge and information are powerful tools. She wanted to make sure that Native Americans have the same access to information on computer networks as other groups.

LaDonna hopes INDIANnet can provide individuals in Native American communities with affordable access to the Internet. Tribes have begun using INDIANnet to communicate with each other and to present themselves on the Internet as they would like the non-Native American world to see them.

INDIANnet gives tribes up-to-date information on issues that are especially important to them. For example, INDIANnet describes programs available from the United States Environmental Protection Agency that can help tribes better protect their lands. INDIANnet is also a place where tribes can learn how other tribes are using technology and the Internet to address problems and to preserve their unique cultures. To help tribes have access to federal government officials and information, INDIANnet has links to the House of Representatives, the Senate, the Bureau of Indian Affairs, Indian Health Services, and other federal agencies.

In 1994 LaDonna served as a member of the

United States Advisory Council on the National Information Infrastructure. This was an important group of advisors who made a report to Vice President Al Gore about what the future of the Internet should be. LaDonna was one of a group of people who strongly believe the Internet should be for everyone.

In 1995 Hazel O'Leary, the Secretary of Energy, appointed LaDonna to the Secretary of Energy Advisory Board. That same year President Bill Clinton appointed her to the board of the Institute of American Indian Arts.

These are just some of the projects that LaDonna hopes will bring the AIO into the 21st century. The AIO will grow and change to meet the needs of native people, no matter what the future brings.

As a leader LaDonna Harris has worked to better the lives of Native Americans and promote the causes of civil rights, women's rights, and the protection of the environment. She has proved that one person can make a difference. She had a dream and the courage and determination to make her dream a reality. Her actions are an inspiration to Native Americans—and to all people who want to make the world a better place.

Out of her many achievements, LaDonna is especially proud of one—her six-year-old grandson, Sam Fred Goodhope. Sam calls LaDonna *Kaqu*, the Comanche term for "grandmother." This is what LaDonna called her grandmother when she was a little girl.

LaDonna has been a friend to many presidents from different political parties, and has had the honor of serving on presidential committees for five of them. Here LaDonna is seen with First Lady Barbara Bush, around 1989.

In Sam, LaDonna sees something she hopes all children will have—the chance to grow up with the values and traditions of their own cultures. She has worked hard so that children everywhere will be able to live a life of possibility and hope for the future.

Important Dates

1931 Born in Temple, Oklahoma.

1949 Marries Fred Harris.

1956 Helps husband, Fred Harris, get elected to the Oklahoma state senate.

1964 Founds the Oklahomans for Indian Opportunity (OIO) Organization.

1970 Founds national organization called Americans for Indian Opportunity (AIO); becomes the first senator's wife to testify before a congressional committee. Because of her testimony, the Taos Pueblo is given back the land around Blue Lake, New Mexico.

1973 Testifies before Congress on behalf of the Menominee tribe of Wisconsin.

1979 Named "Woman of the Year and of the Decade" by *Ladies' Home Journal* magazine.

1981 Divorces Fred Harris.

1994 Appointed to United States Advisory Council on the National Information Infrastructure.

1995 Appointed to the Secretary of Energy Advisory Board and to the board of the Institute of American Indian Arts.

Glossary

attorney general The chief legal adviser of a national or state government.

economic opportunity A way to make a living in order to buy food, clothing, and shelter.

equality All people being treated the same way regardless of race, gender, or religion.

integrate To move into a community of different racial, ethnic, and other groups in order to be treated equally.

landslide An election victory in which a politician receives a far greater number of votes than his or her competitors.

Bibliography

Awiakta, Marilou. *Rising Fawn and the Fire Mystery*. St. Luke's Press, 1984.

Bruchac, Joseph. *Iroquois Stories: Heroes and Heroines, Monsters and Magic*. Crossing Press, 1985.

Ortiz, Simon. *The People Shall Continue*. Children's Book Press, 1987.

Index

American Indian Ambassadors Program, 39–40
Americans for Indian Opportunity (AIO), 32–33, 36–37, 39–44

Carter, President Jimmy, 35
Christianity, 7
Citizen's Party, 36
Civil Rights Movement, 20–21, 25
Clinton, President Bill, 35, 44
Comanche Indians, 6, 10, 15–16, 18, 33, 36, 44

Dust Bowl, the, 13

European settlers, 10–12

Ford, President Gerald, 35

Goodhope, Sam Fred, 44–45
Gore, Vice President Al, 44
Government relocation of Native American tribes, 10–12

Harris, Byron, 38
Harris, Fred, 5, 8, 15, 17–22, 25, 27–29, 35, 38
  Oklahoma State Senate, 18–19
Harris, Kathryn, 38
Harris, LaDonna
  birth, 10
  Civil Rights Movement, 20–21
  divorce from Fred Harris, 38
  father, 6, 10
  first school, 15–16
  grandparents, 6, 15, 18
  growing up, 10, 14–16
  meeting Fred Harris, 17–18
  mother, 6, 10, 14
  move to outside Washington, D.C, 25
  Native American organizations, 36–37
  parents' separation, 14
  speaking to U.S. Senate, 5–6, 8–9
  women's rights, 21–22, 35
  work on various government committees, 35, 44
Harris, Laura, 17, 25, 38, 40

INDIANnet, 43

Johnson, Lady Bird, 26, 34
Johnson, President Lyndon B., 25, 27, 35

Kennedy, Ethel, 27
Kennedy, President John F., 27
Kennedy, Robert F., 26–27
King, Dr. Martin Luther, Jr., 20–21

Ladies' Home Journal, 36
Lawton, Oklahoma, 18, 20

MacDonald, Peter, 30

National Council for Indian Opportunity, 35
National Women's Political Caucus, 35
New Mexico, 5–9, 37–39
Nixon, President Richard M., 9, 30, 35

Oklahoma, 10–19, 21–23, 27
Oklahoma State University, 18
Oklahomans for Indian Opportunity (OIO), 6, 22–25, 28, 31–32

Red Cross, 27
Reservations, 11, 38
Roosevelt, President Franklin D., 17, 19

Segregation, 19–21
Senate Wives Club, 26–27

Taos Pueblo Indians, 5, 7–9, 28
Termination, 28–30
Trail of Tears, 11
Tribal Issues Management System, 33–34
Tribal values, 40–41

University of Oklahoma, 17, 18

War on Poverty, 27–28
Women's Movement, 21–22